The Killing Tree

poems by

J.D. Smith

Finishing Line Press
Georgetown, Kentucky

The Killing Tree

ACKNOWLEDGMENTS

Some of the poems in this collection originally appeared, sometimes in slightly different
form, in the following publications: *Able Muse, Alabama Literary Review, American
Arts Quarterly, Amherst Review, Angle* (United Kingdom) *Anon* (United Kingdom),
*Cadenza (United Kingdom), Construction, Dogwood, Ducts, Light, Measure, New Verse
News, Nimrod, Out of Line, Poetic Voices without Borders 2, Rabbit Poetry* (Australia), *The
Raintown Review, The Rotary Dial* (Canada), *Slice, String Poet, Terrain, Texas Review* and
Think Journal. "Botanical Garden" was reprinted in *Broadsided,* "The Cool of '94" was
reprinted in *Poemeleon* and "Requiem" was reprinted in *Redux.*

"Upkeep" was awarded the 2012 *String Poet* Prize. "Carpe, Carpe" was the June 2010
Goodreads Poem of the Month.

Previous versions of this manuscript were finalists in the following competitions: the *Able
Muse* Poetry Prize, Bright Hill Press Book Contest, the Donald Justice Poetry Prize, the
Richard Wilbur Poetry Award, the *Tampa Review* Prize for Poetry and the T.S. Eliot Prize.

Further acknowledgment is very gratefully made to the National Endowment for the Arts
for financial support, and to the Anam Cara Writer's and Artist's Retreat and the Virginia
Center for the Creative Arts for time, studio space and encouragement in the preparation
of this collection.

Finally, acknowledgment is also very gratefully made to faculty, staff and fellow students at
the West Chester University Poetry Conference and at Poetry by the Sea for their guidance,
support and encouragement, without which this book would not have been possible.

Publisher: Leah Maines
Editor: Christen Kincaid
Cover Art: shutterstock_129566228.jpg
Author Photo: Paula Van Lare
Cover Design: Elizabeth Maines

Printed in the USA on acid-free paper.
Order online: www.finishinglinepress.com
also available on amazon.com

Author inquiries and mail orders:
Finishing Line Press
P. O. Box 1626
Georgetown, Kentucky 40324
U. S. A.

Table of Contents

3.

For Kevin Durkin—friend, colleague, example

Agenda

To renovate the Parthenon,
To know beginnings without end,
To live by bread and bread alone.
To be a string played by the wind.

To raise a pearl outside the shell,
To grow a lemon with no rind,
To learn a useful trade by mail,
To be a string played by the wind.

To write a book-length palindrome,
To walk above the binding ground,
To be, not needing to become.
To be a string played by the wind.

To make my name and make it last,
To be redeemed, not having sinned,
To mold, as clay, bronze long since cast.
To be a string played by the wind.

1.

A Cremation

Fire steals from slow decay the frame
Of one who wished for us to claim
This small relief:

The words are said, the ashes flown.
What's left? A weight, a shard of bone
Still sharp as grief.

Elegy

We weren't allowed the time to contemplate
What talents he in time might come to show,
What fame or wealth he might accumulate,
What love and other passions he might know.

We had, instead, the chance to see him crawl
And graduate to solid food, to take
Some wobbling steps that ended in a fall,
To hand an uncle's dog a piece of cake.

To say more is to claim a flare's bright arc
Could have reached high, though it had scarcely flown
Before dissolving in the larger dark.
We fall back on the facts, which stand alone.

He seldom cried. He used to point at birds.
And now he will be missed beyond all words.

Lullaby for the Bereaved

Your hours of tears won't let you follow
Those who've left you alone.
Tonight your head lies on a pillow,
Not beneath earth and stone.

The dead won't be returning,
Not for all of your pleas,
Nor for all your candles burning.
Get up off your knees.

The deceased, removed from their rest
Can take up all your hours
Until your mind, denied a fair rest,
Is deprived of its powers.

The road set before you is rocky and steep,
So seize the night's respite and drift off to sleep.

Upkeep

Two full-time checks could hardly pay the bills—
and sometimes they still didn't—let alone
prescriptions and more urgent kinds of pills
that soothed, or caused, another broken bone.
The heat went out. Most months it couldn't wait,
no more than the plumbing that would clog and cough
and give out at some ever-faster rate.
The numbers never worked out to take off
the half-hive on an upstairs window-pane.
Its gray curve could be made out from the street.
The flat side, facing in, exposed a grain
of chambers churned by drones and queen, complete
with larvae, eggs, scant honey on the comb,
and all the furtive workings of a home.

Heart

As if it weren't enough to be itself,
A boneless fist evolved—condemned—to clench,
To pump some billion times or so between
The first translucent flutter in the womb
And a sudden stop or stuttering toward death,
The heart is faced with pressure from all sides.
Parts north and south would crown their colleague king
And cause of all their willing and their want.

The heart brooks none of this—it has a job
And isn't looking for another one.
And democratic flattery will fail,
As somewhere in the heart a voice is heard
To say, "If nominated, I will not run
And, if I am elected, will not serve."
For reasons of its own, the heart insists
With every pulse, "Not me. Not me. Not me."

The Promised Land

Next to a clearing in the forest preserve—
Which trailhead was a matter of debate—
The trove was left when someone lost his nerve
As park police came close but didn't confiscate

The stacks of *Playboys* that meant *Penthouse*, too,
Weighed down by six-packs of unopened beer.
We spent a summer tracing every clue
That hinted at the unmapped X of *here*

To turn up empties, rubbers worse for wear,
And glossy paper scraps of orange skin
In puzzle pieces without curves or hair.
To study them meant far more work than sin.

To find the rest required more luck or skill
Than we possessed. I'm looking for them still.

Boarding

My group is called—not first, not last—and now
my patience is rewarded with a wait
inside the jetway with the usual
array of travelers in suits or shorts
and all their gear—until the logjam breaks.
We shuffle forward, ducking through the door
to pause again and size up where we'll go,
or see where others go. First class is full,
cell phones in use before the champagne's poured,
small consolation for the suitcase life.
Two further surges bring me near my row.
The aisle and middle seats are occupied.
The couple shares an in-flight magazine
in which they could be profiled, or be models
persuading us to stay with others like them—
like we would like to see ourselves—at play
in an exclusive luxury resort.
The couple looks that good: both tall, long-limbed
and slender in the ways that make clothes fit
straight off the rack. Their faces are untouched
by surgeons' work, unlined by cigarettes,
uncured by labored tanning and, it seems,
not crossed by crisis great enough to cost
a sense of self, or hope. Without these marks
their faces shine like near-still pools at noon.

Their conversation, heard in bits above
the thump of bags and flight attendants' calls
that penetrate the murmur of the crowd,
is bright with terms like "fellowship" and "post,"

suggesting constellations of good luck
drawn in their shapes and those of first-named friends
they've visited in cities I've seen once
or not at all, all equally beyond
this fiscal quarter and the next, to be
filled with a dozen different trips like this,
for work such as informs no childhood dream.
It took my youth, and more, to get this far.
The couple is already there: point B
attained, they might complete the alphabet.
How far have they come from their own points A,
like mine, unchosen? How fast have they gone?
They might explain themselves as we fly west.

With one more forward pulse, I reach my row,
and as I hoist my roller overhead—
before I think to ask—the couple stands.
A short path cleared for now, I take my place.

Drunkard Watched from an Upper Floor

His weaving adds up to a hapless cloth
on both sides of the street: just short of falling,
he staggers, with a stop to vomit froth.
He'd go far safer if he took to crawling.
A brace of cans, though, and a paper sack
are taking up the hands his legs could use,
as gales inside his head tell him to tack
and sway but hold his cargo fast, to choose
the service of his thirst above all pride
or fear that he might offer easy prey.
The spirits he has taken as his guide
make him loop back to take another way.

Ten minutes pass. He's near where he began,
reminding me of when I've been that man.

To Himself, of a Certain Age

So far, so good for having no work done,
Although your hands aren't fooling anyone.

The seeds of liver spots, now lightly sown,
Will yield a wealth of darkness once they've grown

While nails and skin grow hard to tell apart,
Dull horn to break a manicurist's heart.

Flesh sags that once was overlain with fat.
(This sinking ship's abandoned rat by rat.)

What's left are gnarls of knuckle, flesh and vein
To seize the day in stiffness and in pain.

Your fingers bend into a tightening grip,
With what chance to recover should it slip?

Late Bachelorhood

It was a time of lostness, like the times
that came before, yet sharpened by the thought
that this time might, at length, become the last:
a path that narrows to a point soon lost
like others in horizon and dark distance,
if not a circuit travelled with the hours,
marked off stations of no cross: to work,
a quick meal out, or home, such as it is,
where cooking is not done. And so to bed
until the next day's lap, at slowing pace,
toward prizes known and not set to increase.
The weekend's foretaste of advancing age
was seasoned by the dwindling hours of friends
not called away to children, spouse and yard.
The staple rest was chores, long shifts at bars,
the pleasures possible in solitude
at movies or museums where, sometimes,
the roots of awe held fast against all rote
and lifted up a brilliant, whole, round world
that offered lush abundance, even perfection
when viewed in certain lights. Yet to embrace
that world complete would mean to touch, at most
a poverty of points, at little depth.
To hold more of its bounty would require
a handle and, at length, another hand.

Proposal

Resign yourself, my heart's delight,
To me before a better offer
Comes along with hair and height,
A sea-deep chest, a bulging coffer.

Don't wait for him: if love's a song,
I am the toad's primeval croak.
If love's a wheel, then I belong
Among its rusty, broken spokes

If I mean nothing in the world
To you, that nothing could be all,
A version of transcendence, curled
And primed to blossom from your soul.

Who else is equal to this test,
This cup of gall? You've had a sip—
In our shared life you'll taste the rest.
Come join me on this sinking ship.

Sans Issue

What ends with me? A set of genes,
The notion that my slender means
Might turn into a son's estate,
The hope that, at some distant date,
Beside my grave, my line convenes

To recollect my days' routines,
My counsels, and the vanished scenes
Whose witnesses would recreate
        What ends with me:

The consciousness that struts and preens
In holding that its passing means
An altering of our species' fate,
My thought possessed of untold weight.
Yet, on that thought, the question leans—
        What ends with me?

Epithalamium

For Eric and Arica, 13 November 2004

Whatever one might wish for you today
Already has been wished a hundred times—
Sound health, long years, with children as you please,
Prosperity enough to serve your plans.
Still, we all wish you all these things again
As if, this time, by wishing here assembled,
We might convert fond hope to living fact.
But further still, today we wish for you
Such blessings as we'll never know about:
Mirth in your shared and solitary hours,
Swift compromise on how to spend and save
And, at the heart of all your days, that look
You share across a table or a room
That says again, if silently, "I do."

Upon a Birth

I can't believe you've known this world before
or trust that you will see its light again.
Convention may in this find cause for sorrow.
The same facts can be read with some relief.
Between your age and mine, so many have
already seen too much of what begins
with parents, place and body, all unchosen,
and narrows down from there by chance or choice:
the schoolyard wilderness, the many breaks
implied by ownership of but one heart,
and sometimes worse than all of these combined
the finding of a passion or a gift
too late to tend it unto fruit or flower.
All this is vague, yet I would gladly leave
to your imagination or beyond it
details such as I've drawn in for myself,
or others that will differ and be yours
whatever I may wish on your behalf.
Yet knowing this, I still must wish you all
the years you need to turn into yourself,
a sea of time that cannot wash away,
but may quite well dilute, your share of grief.
May you discern as well, amid your days
the instants brilliant as a gem—or like
a blade—that may be taken up to make
a single life precluding untold others,
and somehow handle each accordingly.
In any case, may you retain some sense
of how a world should be, not only how
it is, or seems, so that the part you shape
serves as a modest template for the rest
wherein the distance from the real to the ideal
is small enough to measure with your laughter.

2.

Fragment from Zeno

Motion's largely an illusion.
Though distances narrow
By halves, then more halves, things remain apart.

While unschooled minds yield to confusion,
The bronze-tipped arrow
Only seems to pierce the roebuck's heart.

Botanical Garden

The trade show done, the flight home well ahead,
The hour too soon to linger in a bar,
We leafed at length through what the brochures said
Might make use of our time and rental car.
Arriving at a point of local pride
And global note, according to its ads,
We bought feed at the pond, then cast it wide
And watched for motion in the lily pads.
First one koi buoyed and snatched its floating dole,
As we had seized a sample or a lead.
Soon others rose, a sudden, mottled shoal;
The water roiled with something more than need.
We threw no more and wished the water clearer:
Less of a feeding frenzy—or a mirror.

Monday in Las Vegas

The skirts are off the tables.
A bucket's on the floor
Until the plumber shows up.
In comped rooms, whales still snore.

An escort takes the day off
For visitation rights.
McCarran's slots are ringing
With scores of outbound flights.

Housekeeping finds stray bits of
What happens and stays here:
Pawn tickets and a red chip,
Three shoes and one brassiere.

Booms or busts in housing
Roll through the neighborhoods,
And long-haul trucks deliver
All necessary goods.

Lit hard against the evening,
Severe and even grand,
The Luxor's daytime profile
Recedes into the sand.

Working Farm for Sale

The hives have gotten through another year—
I'm sure you've heard of the alternative.
Buy soon and you can have the Holsteins here.
No guarantee of how much milk they'll give.

Tobacco had the soil worn out before
Some fallow years and compost brought it back.
The orchard yields enough to eat and store,
Or make a batch of your own applejack.

Of course, a price like this can't buy perfection.
Feel free to ask me questions and take notes.
You get the feed lot's smell from that direction.
The stream is muddied by a neighbor's goats.

Let's step inside. The gun rack's over there.
This far from town, you'll want a gun somewhere.

At a Bistro

A speck adrift in red wine caught my eye
    And took shape as a minute fly,
    Both wings and all six legs aflail
    On alcohol and surface tension
    Before the facts of physics could prevail,
Barring a rarely-offered intervention.

I could have waited for another glass
    (The server, though, would seldom pass)
    Or drunk my order, fly and all,
    But squeamishness surpassed my thirst
    Up to a point: my stomach wall,
I hoped, would hold against stray microbes' worst.

Possessed by curiosity or sloth,
    And probably a bit of both,
    I dipped a spoon into my drink
    And, drawing up a sea-dark sip,
    Spilled out the excess on the zinc
And left the sodden insect on the tip.

The ruby droplet turned to air, the fly
    Held out its wings to further dry
    Until, it seemed, no worse for wear
    Nor swallowed in a drunken haze
    It lifted off into the air
To live out its remaining hours or days.

This flight called for another round.
    No better reason could be found:
    I'd saved a helpless life, although
    In the face of minimal resistance.
    Today I'd nothing else to show
For my bourgeois mock epic of existence.

What grace, in turn, might I hope to receive?
    I paid the check and took my leave.

The Cool of '94

Distraught as if a god had died,
They wept and moaned for Kurt Cobain.
Still, Eddie Vedder was their guide
To plumbing depths of white-bread pain.
"Alternative" had yet to wane.
Doc Martens thudded on the floor.
Perhaps Fox Mulder could explain—
Where are the cool of '94?

Where did the slackers run and hide
Who clerked while on a higher plane?
And where the girls those slackers eyed?
Which still wear Seuss hats and disdain
The suit and tie as ball and chain?
Who still shops at the Goodwill Store?
Can any answer this refrain:
Where are the cool of '94?

Did some leave meth and X untried,
Yet find a world of weight to gain?
Do some sell real estate, or ride
In car pools or a morning train?
Since when did they go with the grain?
When did they wise up, learn the score?
The years' thread spins out from the skein.
Where are the cool of '94?

Like snowflakes melting in the rain,
They've lost their shape and are no more.
We ask our former selves, in vain,
Where are the cool of '94?

Missing a Vigil

I've been to school enough to know the thoughts
I ought to have, and usually I do,
among them, that the State can claim no right
to kill a man who takes another's life.
The arguments buoy up from memory:
two wrongs don't make a right, nor should
the State become a murderer itself.
Besides, how often does that possibility
hold back the trigger finger or the knife?
That highest price, moreover, is exacted
according to the killer's skin or name.

Tonight's rebuttal states its claims in power.
The final stay expired, the date is set
in stone: the governor has guaranteed
he'll make no last-hour call of clemency,
which could impede a bid for higher office.
The first injection starts at 12:01.

The promised outcome doesn't stanch the flow
of envelopes of updates, calls for action,
pleas for donations large and small so that
outrages of this sort will one day end,
backed up by pre-recorded calls
reminding us that we can still bear witness.
This act won't be presented as a thing
done in our names. The calls have several scripts,
including one delivered by a star
who closes with the (ad lib?) valediction
"and let our candles raised in truth speak for
the world that lies beyond the prison walls."
Some will no doubt be raised, as other lights
will celebrate the time of death, regretting
only its late date and dearth of pain.

Both sides will make their voices heard, and find
their pictures in the news, as certainly
as justice, already served, will be exceeded.

These facts are joined by others close at hand,
no more susceptible to argument.
The penitentiary's an hour away.
It's Tuesday night, and tomorrow's nine o'clock
was scheduled before the last appeal.
The car stays in the garage, a choice that stems
from others and confinements they entail,
as debts of all kinds must be paid in full,
if not those to society, for now,
yet those to colleagues, mortgage and a dog
too old to board and needing frequent walks,
one who has earned no kind of punishment.

Envy the Dutiful

after Dana Gioia

Envy the dutiful,
the dogs, the wallflowers,
the prom non-attendees
home at all hours.

Envy the waterboys,
the dweebs and the techies,
the Poindexters born
predestined for wedgies.

The nerds and nerdettes,
the gawky, the scrubs
liked but as "just friends,"
the terminal schlubs.

Envy the bookworms,
unhip, ungainly,
the late-blooming Venus
now sought insanely.

Envy the duds
who've bided their time.
Envy the day
their stock starts to climb.

Urbis

We came from farms, from small towns,
distant countries, and we were various—
the sodomites, the bored,
the bookish and unmarriageable,
and mostly, those who knew
that, wherever they had come from,
the pies had been cut long ago.
We made from level land, fresh water,
a place that would embrace us,
our coin of effort
held in common currency.
From it, docks and bridges rose,
tracks webbed a continent,
a fist of skyline broke the plain.
Our want outlined, we brought it
to a brittle gleam
with theaters and stadia
spreading wide and filling full
of cliques enough for everyone
to find one of his choice,
and others whose postal code,
or skin, made the choice worthwhile.
Only on free evenings
do new wants arise—
to visit parents' graves
and buy a nearby plot,
to have the pleasure of, besides a dog,
the space to let him run.

The Size of Things

Things get smaller as we age,
As verified when we return
To childhood's home—too small a stage,
Too cramped for anyone to learn

A mother tongue, a social grace,
To ride a bike, to add a sum,
But every place remains in place
And states its earthly, firm *I am:*

A once-big desk at once-big school,
A shrunken church, a shrunken store,
An oceanic backyard pool
Diminished at its bluegrass shore.

So here our letters were addressed
Once we had left for brighter lights,
Which we've since seen, and aren't impressed.
The old, familiar smallness blights

The capitals of foreign lands,
Stunts their mountains, tames their wilds.
Repetition comprehends
Our making love, and what it yields.

Such secrets as exist are bared,
And after some score years are done
We're full of time and stand prepared
To face the world to come, or none.

Detox

Gone were the primal fireworks in his head
that held all creeds' enlightenment,
and gone the days when women seemed
to cast their nets and lures for him
without asking for a diamond, or to hear a vow.

If there were, at times,
the sudden zeroes in his bank account,
the weeks that couldn't be recalled, evictions,
that was the price he had to pay
for standing now and then outside himself
and walking, just a bit, above the ground—

until alleged loved ones intervened,
as if a bland salvation could be found
in waking up unsoiled, on time
to man a desk and line a stranger's pockets
for eight hours a day.
He'd held that sober grail before,
clean, empty, and soon smashed it.

If only now his mother were alive,
there might yet be a way
to ask her for forgiveness,
and to bring a flask.

Hero, Posthumous

The safety off. One false move would mean death.
He would not move for nothing. He'd seen death.

Though perfect and rare was the bloody ballet,
The blatant full stop of on-screen death,

More likely were long months on life support,
Dialysis for years, a machine death,

If not memory's decay, a heart lined with plaques,
Or cancer's forced march. An obscene death.

Only an instant to reach for the gun
And shout *God is gracious! A clean death!*

Intimation

It is as when, after leaving for work,
you wonder if the coffeemaker's off.
The thought of unplugging it arose, but then
the dog began to bark at unseen threats.
The keys took an eternity to find.

The morning passes in a blur of words
and pixels overshadowed by the thought
of *Did I flip the switch? And if I didn't?*
Forgetting hurts, like pouring Liquid Plumr®
down aged pipes and forfeiting a whole
security deposit. This time, though,
there's equity at stake. Once the carafe
dries out and cracks, when will the rest catch fire?
How quickly could the house burn down to nothing?

Lunch probably takes place somewhere. Perhaps.
What's certain is the tallying of risks.
Will wanton negligence/boneheadedness
be covered, or was this the place I thought
to save a pittance on the premium?
(The mind is as those old, corroded pipes.)
No payment in the offing, what comes next,
rebuilding or a shedding of all goods?
What are the grounds for making either choice?

At this point everything is on the table.
The table's wobbling on a short, loose leg.

Spinoza at Lenscrafters™

Next. NEXT.
One moment, please, as I review this text.
Let's see. *The universe does not equate with God,*
But God infuses all—
As air and avarice fill up this mall—
As antecedent sunlight will infuse and prod
A bud to flower.
That's good enough. And here's my card, feel free to call.
Though you might find yourself perplexed,
Your glasses will be ready in an hour.

Seven Ages of Man

I puked and cried—that's what Mom said.

School sucks. Why can't I stay in bed?

I want that girl. What is her name?

I'll kick some ass and stake my claim.

I'm fat. So what? I've won the game.

I limp these days, and feel the gout.

Say, now, what was all that about?

To His Skeleton

At length, sharp bone
Becomes well known
As mottled skin
Grows paper thin,
Firm flesh shrinks back
And joints go slack,
As aches diffuse
Their worsening news.

Why excavate
At this late date
What will return
To earth, or burn?
What truth discerned,
What lesson learned
Requires this taste
Of coming waste?

No answers come
From Nature, mum
And still, which bends
To its own ends.
But asking will
Demand its fill.
As bones emerge,
Fresh questions surge.
What's lost, at length,
Besides youth's strength?

Gone like sound knees
Are memories
Of long disease,
Uncertain cure,
Thought turned from pure
At early age
To gnarls of rage
At schoolyard taunts,
The unmet wants
Of single years,
Hard by careers
At lowly tiers
Of grinding gears
Or tapping keys,
And by degrees
Attaining, lo,
A long plateau
From which some fall,
For whom that's all
Until flesh fails,
Bone slips its veils.
This brings us to
The present view
Of short days left
And time's sure theft—
If indiscreet,
Not incomplete.
What's taken, then,
Won't come again,
Which holds, in brief,
Along with grief,
No small relief.

3.

Beginning with a Line from *The Bread Bible*

If working with a sticky dough alarms you,
First make yourself less prone to its effects.
Wash hands and forearms for some time, then dry
So thoroughly that no bits cling or slip.
These measures failing, or bypassing them,
Attempt to work with plastic gloves so that
Each finger's safe in its respective condom,
With all of the attendant loss and gain.
Regardless of the method you select,
Flour surfaces until an arid fog
Is stirred by your least move or slightest breath.
You may then ponder some alternatives:
Not having dough, or hands to knead it with—
Not to mention, as we often don't,
The distant if well-known enormities
That strike the Horn (and heart) of Africa
And everywhere it serves as metaphor,
Details of which can murder appetite.

To step away from melodrama, though,
What is the worst thing that could happen here?
A person learning baking from a book
Can well afford to lose a loaf or two
En route to golden-brown perfection.
The kitchen cleared, trash taken out, that loss
Will not be noted or remembered more
Than taking second in a spelling bee,
Failing a driving test the first time out,
Not getting into Harvard, or Yale Law.
Get over them, yourself, and if you must,
The Buddha in the road. Dough doesn't care.
If such indifference is not to taste,
Still try to raise your threshold of alarm.
Take stock, a breath, a shot of something strong.
Remember the alternatives. Start in.

Requiem

A teddy bear, an *R.I.P.*
Spray-painted on a wall,
An empty bottle mark the place
That saw a young man fall.

His name reads like leftover type
Or random Scrabble tiles
Appearing now, if not before,
In transcripts and case files.

Perhaps a hard look or a word
Translated into beef:
The seed unknown, the harvest come
To customary grief.

What counsel could be offered here
That wouldn't be declined
As some attempt to, once again,
Impose a whiter mind?

From habit, hope or vague good will
Some write checks and some vote.
Awaiting the desired effects
Leaves ample time to note

A teddy bear, an *R.I.P.*
Spray-painted on a wall,
An empty bottle mark the place
That saw a young man fall.

Century of Ideas

Mandelstam transcended them,
As Mayakovsky wished he had.
Rivera broadly painted them,
And Tzara saw his own go mad.

A system that addressed the flesh
Became incarnate in *das Volk*
Who, fulfilling their shared wish,
Translated persons into smoke.

A war's dust, settled, left on hand
Two systems whose dispute revolved
Around a wall that would not mend
Until it was, with words, dissolved.

Now freed from creeds, transactions mount.
Wires thick with funds give flesh to graphs.
What can't be counted doesn't count.
By Hades' beds, Procrustes laughs.

Carpe, Carpe

I'm sawing off the limb I'm on.
A cartoon in a three-D scene,
I'm on this branch until it's gone,

Like men who dam where salmon spawn
To keep a desert golf course green.
They're sawing off the limb they're on,

As I've shirked sleep, as if élan
Were made of gin and nicotine.
I'm on this branch until it's gone,

But poison weeds and feed the lawn
And hope my drinking water's clean,
Still sawing off the limb I'm on,

And sprinting in a marathon
Whose finish line is still unseen.
I'm on that branch until it's gone.

Why work when there are rings to pawn?
We'll live off fat, and then on lean.
I'm sawing off the limb I'm on.
I'm on this branch until it's gone.

Consultative

The noted scholars of the institute
Are tasked with framing issues and debate.
Through data and the values they impute
By proxy—or assume—they correlate

The wealth of nations and their policies,
Distinguishing phenomenon and cause
Until equations cut through fallacies,
Assuming over time the air of laws.

Accordingly, with every factor weighed,
The State will be apprised of how to spend.
In high demand, proportionately paid,
Those who've advanced their field approach day's end

With puzzles yet to solve, but satisfied,
And step around the beggars stretched outside.

Citizen Vain

Rosebud

Who burned his sled? That would explain
The wisps of hair coiffed like a mane,
The name writ large on thrusting towers,
His rating of his works and powers.
Who wouldn't take up his refrain?

A loser, say, without a brain
And envious he can't obtain
Fresh wives imported like cut flowers.
   (Who burned his sled?)

A nation may endure a reign
Of fire once tended with some pain
Outlasting its appointed hours
Yet starved, for all that it devours.
The question holds fast like a stain—
   Who burned his sled?

The Killing Tree

Here drive the nail.
Here set the noose.
Draw poisons from
The leaves' harsh juice.

Its lashing thorns
Cut to the bone.
Its bark as hard
As paving stone,

It thrives in loam
And rocky ground.
Its shade is deep,
Its stern limbs bound

For sharp-tipped stakes,
For shaft and stock—
They hold no nest
And shield no flock.

With all the seeds
Its black fruits hold,
It multiplies
A thousand fold.

After an Injustice

Ferguson

My silence does not mean assent
Or celebration of a wrong.
Enough will say, in the event,
The arc of history is long . . .

May those most wounded as it bends
Be heard before another voice,
For sympathy or lesser ends,
Pollutes the central cry with noise

As if right words could outweigh blood
Or stay a tide, and then a flood.

Invocation

Of arms and of great men I'd like to sing,
Of war unleashed by beauty and sustained
By pride and wrath unto a city's end,
A shipwrecked trickster, general and king
Condemned to exile of long wandering,
A soldier of the vanquished side who found
And fathered forth an even greater land,
For singing of this kind can ease death's sting.

But these aren't epic times. Command lies far
From bravery and seeks, above all, rent.
If genius shirks from doing what it must,
May talent's work suffice to make a tour
Of time and place to fairly represent
The spirit now indwelling future dust.

Two Capitals

1. Athens

Life must have smelled more then.
Along with dung and dust,
the urine sluicing through the tanneries
and cheeses going bad in the Agora,
the strigil-scraped and rancid oil
from wrestlers' backs, like resined wine
and roasting joints of lamb,
would have suffused the air, if not enough
to banish sweat.

Those scents dispersed, what's left?
Besides orations, plays, ceramics,
some verse, inquiries on
the nature of the Good, presided over by
a temple whose proportions cast
a shadow on the works
of every generation that has followed.

2. District of Columbia

The present's odor, though
noxious with exhaust,
or polysyllables of nitrogen
that manure far-sprawling fields,
may waft more faintly in comparison,
a benediction or achievement of
refrigerators and the vaccines they can hold,
and sewerage that leads unglamorously
to health, thus widening the canopy of years
beneath which we draw breath,
find entertainment, undertake
perhaps some larger task.
Above the buried genius of the Metro,
one or another borrowed idiom prevails
in castle, column, obelisk,
and an accounting made of wishes more than means
while texts of native wisdom fray
or turn to fossils under glass.
A later age may find, in this, our scent.

Federal District

In Lanyard Land the young aspire,
With fresh degrees and selfless fire,
    To shape the policy debate
    And steer aright the ship of state
The old have run aground in mire.

Fact sets a limit on desire.
To have a voice, one must acquire
    The means and friends that carry weight
In Lanyard Land.

When wisdom fails to find a buyer,
Agendas turn to who will hire
    Those left outside the narrow gate.
    Indentured at the going rate,
Those who were young wait to retire
In Lanyard Land.

At the United States Navy Memorial

The shattered man proclaims a cryptic cause.
So far he hasn't broken any laws.
While pacing in a cloud of words and smell
The shattered man proclaims a cryptic cause
As tourists pass. One says "He isn't well"
And doesn't stop, for all he has to tell.
The shattered man proclaims a cryptic cause.
So far he hasn't broken any laws.

Washington Memoir

Now the truth can be told—it's about me.
Since my birth, all who've known me would tout me.

The top firms all needed to scout me.
One man put opponents to rout: me.

At Vail, who caught the most trout? Me.
(Here's a picture at prayer of devout me.)

Wealth found—with prestige and clout—me,
Whose counsel was always sought out? Me.

Only fools, knaves and cynics would doubt me.
No wonder I can't help but shout *ME!*

Inquest

The flesh is breached,
The venom spread,
The heart's core reached,
The victim dead.

Attention then
Turns to a cause.
What beast again
Might bare its claws?

What hand might wield
A doubled spike,
One still concealed
And set to strike?

A board convenes,
Investigates
The motives, means
And ending, states

That policies,
If well-defined,
Need not appease
The common mind.

Thus panels form
To formulate
A law or norm
To forge a state

That would preclude
The thought of wrath—
Or set the mood
To seek that path.

As plans abound
And measures crawl
That gain no ground
Fresh victims fall,

And some perceive
They hear a word
Or may believe
A voice inferred

From field and brake
As rattles shake:
Make no mistake.
There is no snake.

The Light on the Dome

*On the eve of Constantinople's fall, Emperor Constantine Palailogos
writes to Anna Notaras, to whom he was once engaged.*

Don't band an answer to the pigeon's leg.
In fact, don't send him back to me at all.
My lowest subject won't be made to drink
The cup I've passed, the dwindling life of waste
That drains away from rulers who survive
Their reigns, to bear captivity at home,
Abroad the prison of the common lot.
This is the pain of amputees, or better,
Eunuchs whose fleshy capon steps and floating
High notes of speech recite their vanished grandeur.
The bird's puffed chest would exhale all his pride
If he should find an empty palace, or
One full of strangers, which is all the same.
That future shades into our land's fatigue;
For weeks no child has come to light alive.
We've lost the hope of generation—hens
Lie tight as white, drawn purses; goats run dry.
An animal sense makes them wait until
The ground shifts from one owner to another.

The foss is filling. With one breach, inside
And out will merge, and merged, will cease to be.
Its dust descends to claim the dynasty.
Our book is closing on its years of bulk;
The Turkish cannon mark the final jots.

And next? No one can guess. The future's all
One great estate that never finds its lord.
They'll take more lands and use another name
For God, and dare the curse this city gives
Its rulers like a poison from a well.
Forgive me if I ramble, but behind
These walls the lilies of the field would toil
If forethought shook their stems; their blooms will fall

By scythes of crescent flag and scimitar—
Reduced to dusty gray, the same as grass
That wilts and frames their pride with lowly contrast.

At twilight, in accordance with the oracles
Of our last day, a most peculiar light
Shrouded the Hagia Sophia's dome.
It always seemed another widows' fable, like
The luck of eating bread inlaid with coins
On New Year's Day. Who heeds a prophecy
Until it's true? Today I knelt low as
A flagstone when the icons were paraded through
The streets, then knew I'd soon be entering
The sea of ages that begin to lap
Across this land and take us, like Atlantis,
To Chaos whence it came. Like one who stands
Above our straits, where continents lie near
But never meet, I see two periods,
The gulf between that battle's bones can't fill.

Defeat and victory retreat in thought.
We fight as if against the sun's sure fall
To prove our city's worth, a kingdom's blood.
The flag may fall, but I'll retrieve its honor.
The ransom is myself, a king, a man
Whose manhood lies in obligation met.
That memory will give a lonely pride
To slaves, whose pasts deny a master,
And exiles who will follow sunrise west.
Before this reaches you, I will have gone
Beyond the Sultan's rule. He often sets
The vanquished head, a trophy, on a plate.
I'll yield that much—I'm hardly greater than
The Baptist—but a head that never bowed.

A kingdom must be built from such omissions.

Along the Potomac

An eagle rides the thermals for a time,
Encircling an invisible sublime
Or turning in a random, slow descent—
Then plunges to a place where light is bent
By currents thick with both life and debris,
Emerging from the low point of a V
With talons holding fast a fingerling,
Which draws by sight or scent, as by a string,
From trashcan, monument and splintered dock
Wide-scattered gulls into a moment's flock
Until they take the prey or make it fall
Into its native water, lost to all.

Each bird, as it is shaped, pursues its ends.
Upon their flights and nothing else depends
The battle, yet one watching from the ground
According to his nature, too, is bound—
In vain—to take a side, then justify
The choice, pretending that his tastes supply
A judgment representing higher laws
Than those administered by beaks and claws.

Seen in this light, gulls live on every food
Where garbage-heaps sustain their multitude
While, in a narrow niche, the raptor needs
Live flesh—and may be poisoned, as it feeds,
By substances first spread to raise the yields
Of row crops grown for feed in upstream fields.

The outcome still unknown, one might well stay
And cheer in silence for the bird of prey.

J.D. Smith has published three previous collections, *Labor Day at Venice Beach* (2012), *Settling for Beauty* (2005), *and The Hypothetical Landscape* (1999). His books in other genres include the humor collection *Notes of a Tourist on Planet Earth* (2013), the essay collection *Dowsing and Science* (2011), and the children's picture book *The Best Mariachi in the World* (2008). Awarded a Fellowship in Poetry from the National Endowment for the Arts in 2007, he has also been a fellow at the Virginia Center for the Creative Arts.

His individual poems have appeared in *The Able Muse, American Arts Quarterly, Dogwood, Light and Nimrod*, as well as numerous other publications, and his prose has appeared in *Boulevard, Chelsea, The Laurel Review* and *The Los Angeles Times*. Born in Aurora, Illinois and educated at American University, the University of Chicago, Carleton University and the University of Houston Creative Writing Program, he works as an editor and writer in Washington, DC, where he lives with his wife Paula Van Lare and their rescue animals.

www.ingramcontent.com/pod-product-compliance
Lightning Source LLC
Chambersburg PA
CBHW021202090426
42740CB00008B/1193